THE WHITE ELEPHANT AND OTHER TALES FROM INDIA

This edition published by Lector House in 2023

ISBN: 978-93-5800-746-6

Lector House LLP
Registered Office: H. No. 96, Block C, Tomar Colony,
Burari, Delhi – 110084, India
info@lectorhouse.com
www.lectorhouse.com

THE WHITE ELEPHANT AND OTHER TALES FROM INDIA

GEORGENE FAULKNER

2023

LECTOR HOUSE LLP

The White Elephant

"No, no," said the Queen....
"I never coax the King to do anything against his will."

THE WHITE ELEPHANT AND OTHER TALES FROM OLD INDIA

RETOLD BY

GEORGENE FAULKNER

"The Story Lady"

ILLUSTRATED BY
FREDERICK RICHARDSON

TO MY RADIO FAMILY
Who, unseen but appreciative,
always request more
Animal Tales

CONTENTS

My Dear Children:

These old, old tales from India have been favorites for many, many years; some have come down to us from the early days of Buddha, and were taken from a book, called the "Jataka Tales," telling of the Buddha's previous existences. Some of these old tales have been translated from the Pali by Eugene Watson Burlinghame, and they have also been retold for us in attractive form by Ellen C. Babbitt.

These stories are somewhat similar to stories which we have all known in another form; for instance, our first story of "The White Elephant" is somewhat like the story of Androcles and the lion. While the story of "The Timid Little Rabbit" is like the old English tale of "Chicken Little."

"The Story of the Grain of Corn" (which is repeated from "Tales of the Punjab" by Flora Annie Steel) compares with our well-known version of "The Old Woman and the Pig." In this same book, we find the story of "The Bear's Bad Bargain," and we learn how a stupid and clumsy bear is outwitted by a grasping old woman and her greedy husband. Even if they have the best of the bargain, our sympathies are all with the poor old bear.

"The King of the Mice," "The Bold Blackbird," and "The Kid and the Tiger" (retold from "The Talking Thrush and Other Tales from India," collected by W. Crooke and retold by W. H. D. Rouse) are all stories of the triumph of the weak and cunning over the brutish and strong. "The Bold Blackbird" may remind you of the old French tale of "Drakesbill and His Friends."

In many of these old tales, the little Jackal is the hero, and, like Reynard the Fox of European folk lore, and our own Bre'r Rabbit in the "Uncle Remus" tales, we find the Jackal through his wit and strategy overcoming the larger, stronger animals.

For example, in the stories of "Singh Rajah and the Cunning Little Jackals," "The Alligator and the Jackal," and "The Brahmin and the Tiger," the Jackal wins his victories by his cunning. These stories of the little Jackal have been retold from "Old Deccan Days" by M. Frere, a most interesting book of tales collected from oral tradition. "The Valiant Chattee-Maker" is also from the same book.

The pictures drawn by our artist, Frederick Richardson, will delight you. Mr. Richardson always makes each illustration true to life: his people dress in the costumes of the country, and his animals are real animals; you can almost hear the big beasts roaring with rage when the little jackal tricks them.

All these tales I have told to you many times over the radio; now I am glad to place them in your own hands to read and retell yourselves.

Your Story Lady.

THE WHITE ELEPHANT

Once upon a time there stood on the banks of a river, near a large forest, a village of Woodcutters. These Woodcutters would go in their boats to the forest and there they would chop down trees. Then they would roll the logs down to the river, and the river would carry the logs to the village, where they were cut into boards and used by the carpenters in building houses and temples.

One day, when the Woodcutters were all busily at work chopping down trees, they heard a great bellowing. A huge Elephant came limping along on three legs, and every little while he gave a great snort.

One of the Woodcutters went up to the Elephant and examined his sore foot. "Come here and help me pull out this big splinter in the Elephant's foot!" he called to the other men. "No wonder the poor fellow is crying with pain."

The Woodcutters all helped. They pulled the splinter out of the Elephant's foot and they brought water from the river and washed the wound carefully. They brought mud from the river banks and spread a mud plaster upon it, and one man tore up his scarf and bound it about the sore foot. Then the men gave the Elephant some food, and he stretched out under the trees to rest.

While he was resting, he watched the Woodcutters at their work. "These men have done so much for me I should like to help them," said the Elephant. So, a few days after that, when his foot was well, the Elephant came again to the place where the Woodcutters were working.

The Woodcutters were cutting down a tree, chop, chop, went their axes and a great tree fell to the ground. Then the Elephant took the log and rolled it over and over until he had pushed it into the river.

"Why, our friend, the Elephant, is helping us with our work!" exclaimed the Woodcutters.

Every day the great Elephant came back. Sometimes he would pull down the trees, and roll them to the water. Other times he would carry the tools for the Woodcutters; and every day the Woodcutters fed him, morning, noon and night, and give him fresh water to drink.

He saved them much hard work and the Woodcutters grew very fond of the big Elephant. He worked for them many years.

Now, this Elephant had a young baby Elephant, who was white all over; and he was very beautiful, indeed.

When the old Elephant saw that his Baby Elephant was strong enough to work, he said to himself: "I must take my son to the Woodcutters, for I am getting old and I am no longer strong. He can learn to do my work and be of service to them."

So the old Elephant said to his son: "White Elephant, now that you have grown large and strong, I want you to help my friends, the Woodcutters. One day, many years ago, when I had a cruel splinter in my foot, they pulled it out for me and bound me up, and gave me food. I have tried to repay their kindness by serving them each day. And each day they give me food and water and are most kind to me. They are my friends and I wish now that you would be friendly with them, also."

So the old Elephant took the White Elephant to the Woodcutters and soon the White Elephant learned to help them, just as his father had done, and they fed him and treated him kindly.

The White Elephant became very friendly with the Woodcutters and every night, when he had finished his work, he would go down on the banks of the river and take a bath and play in the water; and the children of the Woodcutters played with him. Sometimes he would pick the children up in his long trunk and swing them back and forth. Sometimes he would pick them up and put them on his back, and give them a fine ride. And sometimes he would lift them up into the branches of the tall trees.

When it was very warm, he would wade out into the water and take a bath, and often he would take a deep drink of water and then let it out upon the children like a shower bath.

The children loved to romp and play with the White Elephant, and he loved to play with them.

One day the Rajah of the country came down the river and when he saw the White Elephant working for the Woodcutters, he ordered his men to stop while he watched the Elephant. Then the Rajah said:

"I wish to own that Elephant, for I want to ride upon him, myself. He looks so very kind and gentle, and he is very beautiful."

So the Woodcutters had to sell their friend the White Elephant to the Rajah. He paid them a very large price, and then the servants of the Rajah led the Elephant away.

So the old Elephant took the White Elephant to the Woodcutters.

But, as he left the forest, he gave one last look at his playmates, the children, as though he was sorry to say goodbye to them.

The Rajah was so very proud of his beautiful White Elephant he had made for him a robe of crimson velvet embroidered in gold. On his back, the White Elephant carried a throne of gold covered by a gorgeous canopy of cloth of gold.

When the Rajah rode out in great processions he always went upon the back of the beautiful White Elephant. All the days of his life the Rajah cared for the White Elephant, and always the White Elephant served his master, the Rajah, gladly and proudly.

THE GRAIN OF CORN

Once upon a time a farmer's wife was cutting corn in a field when a crow came flying down, swooped off with a bit of the grain and carried it up to a tree to eat it.

The farmer's wife was very angry and scolded loudly:

"You robber, you, to steal my corn!" Picking up a clod of earth, she threw it at the bird with such good aim that the crow fell to the ground, dropping the grain of corn which rolled into a crack in the tree.

The farmer's wife ran up to the crow and, seizing him by the tail, she cried; "You, robber, you! give me back my grain of corn, or I will kill you."

"Caw, caw, caw!" cried the crow. "If you will set me free, I promise to get it for you."

But, lo and behold, when the crow came to search for the corn, it had rolled so far into the crack in the tree that he could not reach it with his beak nor with his claw.

So the poor crow flew off through the forest until he met a woodman and he said:

"Caw, caw! Man, Man! Cut tree,
I can't get the grain of corn
To save my life from the farmer's wife!"

But the woodman refused to cut the tree.

So the crow flew and flew until at last he reached the palace of the king. There were the king and the queen, walking in the courtyard. So the crow flew down to the king and said:

"Caw, caw! King, King! Kill man!
Man won't cut tree;
I can't get the grain of corn
To save my life from the farmer's wife!"

But the king refused to kill the man.

So the crow pulled at the royal robes of the queen, and said:

"Caw, caw! Queen, Queen! Coax king,
King won't kill man;
Man won't cut tree;
I can't get the grain of corn
To save my life from the farmer's wife!"

"No, no," said the queen. "I never coax the king to do anything against his will."

So the crow was very angry and he flew and flew until he met a snake, and he said to the snake:

"Caw, caw! Snake, Snake! Bite queen;
Queen won't coax king;
King won't kill man;
Man won't cut tree;
I can't get the grain of corn
To save my life from the farmer's wife!"

"Hiss-ss! Hiss-ss!" hissed the snake. "I will not bite the queen."

So the crow flew to a stick and said:

"Caw, caw! Stick, Stick! Beat snake!
Snake won't bite queen;
Queen won't coax king;
King won't kill man;
Man won't cut tree;
I can't get the grain of corn
To save my life from the farmer's wife!"

But the stick refused to beat the snake.

So the crow flew on until he saw the fire, and said:

"Caw, caw! Fire, Fire! Burn stick;
Stick won't beat snake;
Snake won't bite queen;
Queen won't coax king;
King won't kill man;
Man won't cut tree;
I can't get the grain of corn
To save my life from the farmer's wife!"

But the fire refused to burn the stick.

So the crow flew and flew until he saw some water, and he said:

"Caw, caw! Water, Water! Quench fire;
Fire won't burn stick;
Stick won't beat snake;
Snake won't bite queen;
Queen won't coax king;
King won't kill man;
Man won't cut tree;
I can't get the grain of corn
To save my life from the farmer's wife!"

But the water ran along as fast as possible and refused to quench the fire.

So the crow flew on until he met an ox, and said:

"Caw, caw! Ox, Ox! Drink water;
Water won't quench fire;
Fire won't burn stick;
Stick won't beat snake;
Snake won't bite queen;
Queen won't coax king;
King won't kill man;
Man won't cut tree;
I can't get the grain of corn
To save my life from the farmer's wife!"

But the ox refused to drink the water.

So the crow flew and flew until he met a rope and said:

"Caw, caw! Rope, Rope! Bind ox;
Ox won't drink water;
Water won't quench fire;
Fire won't burn stick;
Stick won't beat snake;
Snake won't bite queen;
Queen won't coax king;
King won't kill man;
Man won't cut tree;
I can't get the grain of corn

To save my life from the farmer's wife!"

But the rope wouldn't bind the ox.

So the crow flew on until he met a mouse, and said:

"Caw, caw! Mouse, Mouse! Gnaw rope;
Rope won't bind ox;
Ox won't drink water;
Water won't quench fire;
Fire won't burn stick;
Stick won't beat snake;
Snake won't bite queen;
Queen won't coax king;
King won't kill man;
Man won't cut tree;
I can't get the grain of corn
To save my life from the farmer's wife!"

"Ee-EE-Ee-e-e-ee," squeaked the mouse. "I won't help you."

So the crow flew and flew until he met a cat; and he said:

"Caw, caw! Cat, Cat! Catch mouse;
Mouse won't gnaw rope;
Rope won't bind ox;
Ox won't drink water;
Water won't quench fire;
Fire won't burn stick;
Stick won't beat snake;
Snake won't bite queen;
Queen won't coax king;
King won't kill man;
Man won't cut tree;
I can't get the grain of corn
To save my life from the farmer's wife!"

"Miaow! Miaow!" said the cat. "I will—I will." And the moment she heard the word "mouse," she was after it in a rush.

So—

"The Cat began to catch the Mouse;
The Mouse began to gnaw the Rope;
The Rope began to bind the Ox;
The Ox began to drink the Water;
The Water began to quench the Fire;
The Fire began to burn the Stick;
The Stick began to beat the Snake;
The Snake began to bite the Queen;
The Queen began to coax the King;
The King began to kill the Man;

The Man began to cut the Tree;
So the Crow got the grain of corn
And saved his life from the farmer's wife!"

THE TIMID LITTLE RABBIT

Once upon a time there lived a very timid little Rabbit who was always trembling for fear that something terrible was going to happen to him.

One day he went to sleep under a big palm-tree and, when he awoke, he shivered and shook with fright, and said, "What if the earth should fall in? What would become of me, then?"

Just at that very moment, some monkeys up in the tree dropped a big cocoanut. It fell down with a bang upon the ground.

"Oh, dear me! oh, dear me! what a terrible noise!" gasped the little Rabbit. "Oh, dear me! the earth is falling in. Where shall I run and hide?" and the little Rabbit ran bouncing away through the jungle. He never looked behind him to see what had made the noise; he just ran on and on in a panic of fear.

Another little Rabbit saw him running and called out, "Why do you run so fast—and where are you running?"

"Oh, don't ask me, for I cannot stop to tell you," he shrieked, as he galloped along.

The second little Rabbit ran by his side saying, "Tell me! Tell me! What is the matter!"

"Run, run!" gasped the first little Rabbit. "The earth is falling in. The earth is falling in, and I am running away."

So the second Rabbit ran as fast as he could go.

And soon they met another frightened Rabbit, and then they were joined by another and another, until there were hundreds of them, running as fast as they could go, and all shrieking out, "Run! Run! The earth is falling in! The earth is falling in!"

They passed a Deer and the Deer called out, "Where are you all running, and what is the matter?"

"Run! Run!" they cried in terror. "The earth is falling in! The earth is falling in!"

"Oh, oh, where shall we run?" cried the Deer, wildly, for deer are always very timid creatures. And the Deer bounced away after the rabbits.

Next they met a Fox and when he barked out, "What is the matter? Where are you running?" they called to him, "Run! Run! Brother Fox! The earth is falling in! The earth is falling in!"

So the Fox ran with them.

On and on they ran—faster and faster—until they met a Camel and the Fox called out, "Run! Run! Brother Camel! The earth is falling in! The earth is falling in!" So the Camel ran with them.

On and on, they ran, faster and faster, until presently they met a big Elephant. He snorted at them through his long trumpet. "Why do you all run so fast, and where are you going?"

"Run! Run! Brother Elephant! The earth is falling in! The earth is falling in!" called the Camel.

So the Elephant joined them and went madly rushing along through the jungle, blowing a blast through his trumpet and shouting, "Run! Run! The earth is falling in! The earth is falling in!"

Presently they met a big Lion and when he saw them all running in a wild panic, he roared in a loud voice three times, "Grr-rr! Grr-rr! Grr-rr! Stop at once, I command you, and tell me the meaning of this!"

Now this big Lion was the Rajah Lion and he ruled over all the animals in the jungle, so that, when he ordered them to stop, they all stopped at once, and stood still, quivering with fright.

"What is this that you are crying out, and why were you all running in such a panic?" roared the Lion.

"Oh, great and mighty Rajah," they answered, "the earth is falling in and we are running away to save our lives!"

"But if the earth is falling in, how then can you run from it?" asked the Rajah Lion. "I see no signs to show that the earth is falling in. How do you know this, Brother Elephant?"

"Why, I did not know it myself, but Brother Camel told me," answered the Elephant.

"Brother Camel, how did you hear that the earth was falling in?" asked the Lion.

"Run! Run! The earth is falling in."

"Why, I did not hear it myself, but Brother Fox told me," answered the Camel.

"How do you know this, Brother Fox?" asked the Lion.

"Why, I did not hear it myself, but the Deer told me," answered the Fox.

"How do you know this, Brother Deer?"

"Why, I did not hear it myself, but the Rabbits told me," answered the Deer.

"Little Rabbits—little Rabbits," said the Rajah Lion, "how do you know that the earth is falling in? Who told you this?"

Then each Rabbit pointed his paw at another Rabbit and said, "That Rabbit told me."

Finally the Lion asked the little Rabbit who had first told the tale, "Is it true that you are the one who first cried out that the earth is falling in?"

"Yes, Mighty Rajah," answered the little Rabbit, trembling with fear.

"Why, Brother Rabbit, what made you say that the earth is falling in? Is that the truth?" roared the Lion.

"Oh, yes, Mighty Rajah," answered the little Rabbit. "I was asleep under a palm-tree and I awoke in fright and thought 'What would become of me if the earth should fall in?' Then, right behind me I heard a terrible bang! I was afraid to look around, for I knew that the earth was falling in. And so I ran away as fast as I could."

"Well, little Rabbit," said the Rajah Lion, "since you started all this running, you must come back with me to the place where you heard the sound, and we will see if the earth is falling in. All you other animals, wait here until we come back."

So the big strong Rajah Lion took the timid little Rabbit upon his back, and away they went through the jungle. When they came to the very tree where the little Rabbit had slept, the Lion looked all about and there upon the ground he saw the large cocoanut which the monkeys had dropped from the tree.

"Oh, you foolish little Rabbit, it was the sound of this large cocoanut falling upon the ground that you heard. Now, you see that the earth is not falling in. We must go back and you must tell all the other animals the truth," said the Lion.

When they came back to the place where the animals were waiting, the little Rabbit stood before all the animals and said, "The earth is not falling in; the noise that I heard was made by a big cocoanut falling to the ground. I was so startled that I did not look to see what had happened. I am sorry that I frightened you, for the earth is not falling in."

The animals all began to repeat this, and they ran away through the jungle, saying to themselves:

"The earth is not falling in! The earth is not falling in!"

SINGH RAJAH AND THE CUNNING LITTLE JACKALS

Lion

Once upon a time there lived in a jungle a great lion. He was so strong a lion that he had made himself Rajah of all the jungle. Every day when this Rajah lion was hungry he would come out from his cave in the deep dark rocks, and roar in an angry voice:

"Grr-rr-rr! Grr-rr-rr! Grr-rr-rr! Come here, all you animals in this jungle! You are all my subjects, and I will eat you up! Grr-rr-rr, Grr-rr-rr!"

Then all of the frightened little animals would run here, there and everywhere, trying to hide from the angry lion. But Singh Rajah would always catch them and eat them for his dinner.

Now, this went on for a long, long time until at last he had left no living creatures in the jungle except two little jackals, a Rajah Jackal and a Ranee Jackal, who were husband and wife.

"What do you mean?" growled the great Singh Rajah.... "I am the king of this jungle."

These two little jackals were so frightened that they ran here, there and everywhere, trying to get away from that Rajah Lion. But every day he came nearer and nearer.

"Oh dear! oh dear!" moaned the poor little Ranee Jackal; "I am frightened to death. Don't you hear him roaring louder and louder? He is much nearer us today than he was yesterday. Where shall we hide?"

"Never fear, my dear," answered her husband, the Rajah Jackal. "I will take care of you. Let us run another mile or two. Come now, run fast! Come, come!" And they would run on and on through the jungle as fast as they could.

They grew more tired and weary every day, and at last the little Ranee Jackal said, "Oh dear! oh dear! I must stop. I really cannot run another step. I am just worn out."

"Never fear, my dear," answered her husband, bravely. "I will take care of you! Never fear!"

"Oh dear! oh dear!" gasped she, "I hear him coming nearer and nearer. How loud his roaring sounds! He is in a terrible temper and he will surely catch us and eat us today. Oh dear! oh dear!"

"Never fear, my dear!" said the brave little Rajah Jackal. "Come with me and do just what I tell you, and we can save ourselves. Do not look so frightened. Cheer up! Now, come with me, and we will go right up to that lion."

And what did those cunning little jackals do but take hold of paws and go prancing boldly right up to the lion.

When he saw them he began to shake his mane about and his eyes glowed with anger as he roared out, "Grr-rr-rr! Grr-rr-rr! You miserable little wretches! Come here and be eaten at once! I have had no dinner for three whole days, and I am very hungry. I am the Rajah of this jungle, and I have called and called you, but you did not come. And I have run and run to catch you while you have always run away, you miserable little jackals, leading me on and on over hill and dale. Come here and be eaten at once! Grr-rr-rr! Grr-rr-rr! Come here-re-re!" And the Rajah Lion gnashed his teeth and looked very terrible indeed. "Grr-rr-rr! Why didn't you come before?"

"Oh, great Singh Rajah," answered the brave little Jackal, "we do know that you are our master, and we would have obeyed your voice and come at your call long ago, but, indeed, Sire, there is a much bigger Rajah than you in this jungle. For many days he has tried to catch us and eat us, and we are so afraid of him that we have run and run, trying to find a place to hide."

"What do you mean?" growled the great Singh Rajah. "I am the king of this jungle. There is no king here but me."

"Ah, Sire," answered the jackal, "in truth, one would think that you were the king, for you are most terrible. Your very voice is death. But, indeed, there lives a horrible lion in this jungle. His eyes glow like fire. His step is as thunder, and his power is supreme. We have seen him with our own eyes, and he is as much larger than you, as you are larger than we are. Oh, he is indeed most terrible! When he roars his voice is so loud that the leaves tremble upon the trees. He is far more fearful than you!"

"That is impossible!" roared the Lion. "But show me this Rajah who has so terrified you, and I will destroy him at once. I will show you how quickly I can overpower him, and, after I have eaten him, I will eat you!"

Then the little Jackals ran on and on through the jungle with the great lion following them until they reached a very deep well of water. They cowered down beside the well, looking very frightened, while the Rajah Jackal pointed down into the water with his paw, and whispered in an excited little voice, "See, Sire! Look down there!"

The great Singh Rajah came close to the well and, peering down into the water, he saw a great lion's face peering up at him. He was very angry. He shook his great mane, and his eyes glowed like flaming fire, as he roared and roared.

Then the shadow lion shook his mane. His eyes were glowing and he opened his mouth to roar.

"Gr-rr-rr!" roared the Rajah Lion.

"Gr-rr-rr!" answered the echo of his voice from the well.

"Come out of your den and I will show you who is ruler here," roared the lion, gnashing his teeth in rage. But the echo mocked him, and the lion in the well gnashed his teeth.

Now, Singh Rajah was so angry that he could not wait to fight that other lion. So, with a terrific roar, he jumped into the well to kill him.

The well was so deep and the sides were so steep that the great Singh Rajah could not climb out to punish the two little Jackals, who peeped down at him from the top of the well.

Now, when the little jackals knew that he was drowned, they danced round and round the well, singing, "Ao! Ao! Ao! the King of the Jungle is dead. We have killed the great Lion who would have killed us! Ao! Ao! Ao! Ring-a-ting, Ding-a-ting, Ding-a-ting, Ring-a-ting! Ao! Ao! Ao!"

THE KINGDOM OF MOUSELAND

Long, long ago and far, far away, there lived in a forest many, many little mice. They had a wonderful city of their own with their own little shops and churches and a beautiful large palace for their King. Each little mouse had his own little house, with his own little chairs and tables and beds and everything complete. And they all lived very happily in their Kingdom of Mouseland, until one day a terrible thing happened to them. A great caravan came through the kingdom, and none of the men in the caravan knew that their camels were trampling down the forts and big buildings of Mouseland. To them these buildings looked like mounds of sand and Mouseland seemed like any other part of the forest.

So these men, on the backs of the big camels, not knowing what great havoc they were working with the mice, encamped in Mouseland for the night.

One of the Camels became sick and, as the owner thought that it was going to die, he left it in the forest and went on with the caravan. But the Camel did not die. Very soon he got well and, when he was well, he became very hungry. So he strolled all about Mouseland, eating up the crops of the Mice, and treading down their houses until at last he came to the Mouse King's park. He ate a great many trees and trampled down the grass and flowers; and the Keeper ran in a hurry to tell the King.

"Ee-ee-ee-ee!" squeaked the Keeper. "Oh, King, great King! there's a large mountain several miles high out in our garden, eating everything up that is within sight. What shall we do?"

"We must make an example of this mountain," said the King, "or the whole earth will be moving and we shall all be destroyed."

Then the King called to his Prime Minister who was a Fox, named Sandy. "Go, and command that mountain to come to me at once!"

So Sandy, the Prime Minister, went to find the mountain. And the next day he came back, leading the Camel by his nose-string. But, when the Camel saw how very little the King of the Mice was, he began to grunt and to gurgle, to wrinkle up his nose and make scornful faces at the King.

"Hello, is this little thing your King? I thought that your King was a lion at least. I should never have come for such a tiny creature. Bah! you are no more than a speck." Then he turned about and stamped out of the court, eating everything that came in his way.

What could the King do? He was very, very angry, but he had to swallow his wrath and make the best of it. However, he made up his mind that he would take revenge.

And one day, the Camel's nose-string became caught in a creeper so that he could not get away.

Then Sandy, the Fox, came along and he laughed, "He-he-he! You are at our mercy now. He-he-he!" And away ran the Fox and told the King.

The King came with the Fox and when he found that the Camel was a prisoner he said, "Oh, Camel, boastful Camel, you despised my words and now see the result of your wickedness. You are punished for your sins."

"Oh, mighty King," said the Camel very humbly, for he knew now that he was caught, "I do indeed confess my fault and I pray you to forgive me. I will be your faithful servant from now on, if you will only save me."

The Mouse King was not spiteful and, as soon as he heard the Camel beg for forgiveness, his heart grew very soft and he said, "Camel, oh, Camel, I will set you free but hereafter you shall be my servant."

Then the little Mouse climbed up on the creeper and gnawed, and gnawed through the Camel's nose-string and set the camel free.

The big Camel kept his word and he became the servant of the Mouse King. He was so big and strong that he could carry loads which would have needed thousands of Mice, and so he could do more work in one day than a whole army of Mice could do in a week.

The Mouse King commanded the Camel to build strong walls and forts around the city and to make everything so strong that he had no fear of his enemies.

For a long, long time, things went on very smoothly, but one day some Woodcutters came into the forest. These men lived in a strong village of their own and they used the forest wood to build houses. When anyone wanted a new house, the Woodcutters went into the forest and chopped down trees, sawed them into planks, and built a house.

Now, in the course of their wanderings, the Woodcutters found the stray Camel. They seized him and carried him away to serve them by drawing wood.

"Pooh! You silly little mouse," laughed the Woodcutters.... "Come and get your Camel if you want him."

When Sandy told the King that their Camel was caught by the Woodcutters, the Mouse King sent the Fox with a bodyguard to bring the Woodcutters to him. Two of the Woodcutters came before the King, but when they saw the tiny Mouse King, they laughed in his face and mocked him.

"I demand that you return my Camel at once!" squeaked the Mouse King.

"Pooh! You silly little Mouse," laughed the Woodcutters. "Come and get your Camel if you want him!"

"That is what I will do," said the Mouse King. "You may tell your Chief that I will make war upon him unless he gives me back my Camel."

Then the Mouse King called his subjects—millions and millions of them—and they all set out for the village of the Woodcutters.

The Woodcutters had just finished their work and they had been paid a good sum of money, so they were all feeling very happy.

Now the tiny Mice were not able to meet the big Woodcutters out in the field, and fight them, but they had their own way of waging warfare. Night and day, day and night, they burrowed and burrowed under the earth. First they gnawed under the treasury, where no danger was expected; and, one by one, they carried off every coin until it was all empty. Then they burrowed underneath all the houses in the village. Millions of Mice were busy all day and all night, carrying out little baskets of earth from under the foundations. They worked and worked and they gnawed and gnawed, until very soon the Woodcutters' village was standing on a thin shell of earth, while underneath them was a big dark hole.

At last the Mouse King felt that the time had come to strike a blow. He knew that the crust of earth was so thin that the least shock would destroy it. So the Mouse King wrote a letter to the Woodcutter Chief asking once more for his Camel. And in this letter he hid a small package of snuff. He put the letter in the mail and then all of the Mice went away and waited.

When the postman brought the letter to the Woodcutter Chief, he read it through and laughed heartily.

"Ha-ha-ha! that's a good joke. His majesty, the Mouse King, demands that I send back the Camel, or he will wage war against us. Well, let him come on. We will soon wipe the Mice from the face of the earth."

He waved the letter in the air and said, "Let them come on at once!"

Now, as he waved the letter about, all the snuff fell out of it and flew up his nose.

"Kerchoo-Kerchoo-Kerchoo-oo!" sneezed the Chief. And "Kerchoo-Kerchoo-Kerchoo-oo!" sneezed all the men who were near him.

They sneezed so loud and so long that the house shook. The thin crust of earth under them trembled and gave way, and all the Woodcutters fell in, and all the houses in the village tumbled and sank down into the deep dark hole.

After this victory, the Mouse King led his Camel and his army back to Mouseland where they lived in peace the rest of their lives.

THE ALLIGATOR AND THE JACKAL

Once upon a time, a hungry little Jackal went down to the river-side to catch crabs for his dinner. Now, it chanced that in this river there lived an ugly old Alligator, who, being very hungry himself, would have been glad to catch and eat the Jackal. The Jackal ran up and down the bank, hunting for crabs.

He was so hungry that he did not look about cautiously. Had he done so, he might have seen that ugly old Alligator, lying half hidden under some tall bulrushes. So, when the hungry Jackal saw a crab sidling along, he poked his paw down into the water.

Snap! the old Alligator caught the paw of the Jackal.

"Oh, dear, oh, dear!" cried the little Jackal to himself. "What shall I do now? This ugly old Alligator has caught my paw, and soon he will drag me down under the water and eat me."

But the Jackal sang out in a cheerful voice, "Clever Mr. Alligator! Clever Mr. Alligator! I hope you will find that hard old bulrush root tender and you will enjoy chewing on it for dinner."

The Alligator was so buried in the mud under the bulrushes that he could hardly see. He thought that he had made a mistake and he said to himself, "Dear me, how very tiresome! I thought I had caught the Jackal's paw when I had only seized a bulrush root. And there is that saucy little Jackal up on the bank mocking me." So the Alligator opened his jaws and let the Jackal go.

"Oh, wise Mr. Alligator! Wise Mr. Alligator! Thank you for letting me go!" laughed the Jackal. "So you really believed my paw was a root? Thank you, Mr. Alligator!"

Now, when the Alligator found that he was tricked in this way, he was very angry, and he went swimming away, lashing the water to a foam with his tail, while the Jackal hurried up the bank.

The next day the Jackal returned to the river to catch crabs for his dinner. But this time he was very cautious. So he called out, "Whenever I go fishing for my dinner, I see the nice little crabs crawling up through the mud, then I reach down and catch them and eat them. Oh, how I wish that I could see a nice little crab!"

The old Alligator was buried in the mud at the bottom of the river and he heard every word, so he popped out the point of his snout, saying to himself, "That Jackal will take the tip of my nose for a crab and, when he puts his paw down to catch me, I will gobble him up."

But, of course, when the Jackal saw the tip of the Alligator's nose, he called out, in a saucy voice, "Ha, ha! my friend! So that is where you are hidden! I am glad to know where you are. Thank you, wise Mr. Alligator! I will not take my dinner with you today."

And the little Jackal ran barking up the bank as fast as he could go, while the old Alligator lashed the water to a foam with his tail.

On the following day the old Alligator hid himself in the bulrushes close to the bank of the river. He was determined to catch that saucy Jackal.

When the Jackal was hungry for his dinner, he went again to the river to catch crabs. This time, he was very cautious; he went peering all around. He was really much afraid of that old Alligator. However, he called out in a loud and cheerful voice:

"Where have all the nice little crabs gone today? I do not see one, and I am so hungry! Even when they are down under the water I can see them blow bubbles. All the little bubbles go, 'Pop! pop! pop!'"

When the Alligator heard this, he laughed to himself, "I will pretend to be a little crab and blow bubbles; but, when that Jackal puts in his paws, I will catch him and gobble him up!"

So the Alligator began to blow bubbles. "Puff, puff, puff! Bubble, bubble!" But, of course, the bubbles he blew were very large bubbles. They rushed to the top of the water and burst there—"POP! POP! POP!"

As soon as the Jackal saw those big bubbles, he ran away as fast as he could go, calling out, "Thank you, kindly, Mr. Alligator! Thank you! I am glad to see by the bubbles just where you are hidden in the mud. I would not have come here had I known that you were still around."

The Alligator was so angry that he lashed the water to a foam with his tail. "I will not be tricked again by that saucy Jackal," he said. "Next time, I will be as cunning as he is and catch him at his own game."

The Alligator waited for the Jackal many, many days, but the Jackal did not return to the river.

"Who knows," said the Jackal to himself, "but another time that greedy old Alligator will gobble me up. I will not go fishing for crabs any more. I will eat wild figs after this."

So the Jackal stayed in the jungle and ate wild ripe figs for his dinner.

When the Alligator found out that the Jackal did not come down to the river for crabs, he was very angry. "I will follow that rascal up on the land and catch him next time," he said.

And the Alligator crawled and crawled up on the land, dragging his long body through the jungle until he came to the largest fig tree. Here he collected a pile of wild figs and buried himself under them to wait for the Jackal.

After a while the Jackal came scampering into the jungle. But when the little rascal saw the huge pile of wild figs on the ground, he said, "Aha, that looks as though someone was buried under it. Maybe my friend, the Alligator, is under those figs."

And so the Jackal called out cheerfully:

"The nice juicy wild figs I like to eat tumble about on the ground as the wind blows them. This great pile of figs is so still I am sure they are not good to eat. No! I will not eat those figs."

"How suspicious the Jackal is, to be sure," said the Alligator to himself. "But if he wants to see figs tumble about I can make them, and when he comes to eat them, I will catch him and gobble him up." So the great beast shook himself and all the figs went, rolling right off his back, farther than any blustering wind could have blown them, and the Jackal could see the leathery back of the Alligator. So he scampered away, calling out mockingly:

"So kind of you, Mr. Alligator, to let me know just where you are buried under that great heap of figs. No! I don't believe that I want to eat any figs today."

The Alligator was so angry that he snapped his jaws and gnashed his teeth with rage. He ran after the Jackal as fast as he could go but, of course, a big Alligator cannot crawl very fast on his short legs, and the Jackal ran so much faster that the Alligator had to give up the chase. But he said to himself:

"I will not allow that tricky little wretch to mock me and run out of my reach in this way. I will show him that I can be just as cunning as he is."

So, early the next morning, the old Alligator crawled as fast as he could to the Jackal's den and crept into it and hid himself to wait for the little Jackal to come home.

The Alligator was so angry that he lashed the water to a foam with his tail....

When the Jackal came near to his den, he thought, "Dear me! dear me! The ground is all torn up about here as though some great heavy creature had been crawling over it, and the earth is knocked down at the side of my door as though some big animal had been pushing through it. I certainly will not go into my den until I am sure that everything is safe there."

Then the little Jackal began to call out in a sweet voice, "Little house, my pretty little house! Why do you not answer me when I call? When all is safe and right you always call out to me and welcome me back home. Is anything wrong today, little house, that you will not speak to me?"

When the Alligator heard this, he said, "If that is true I'd better call out, so he will know that all is right in his house." And, in a very gentle voice, the Alligator murmured, "Welcome home, sweet little Jackal! Welcome home!"

Upon hearing this the frightened Jackal thought, "Oh, oh! That dreadful old Alligator is in my house. Well, I will surely kill him this time, or he will catch and kill me."

Then the Jackal answered, very sweetly, "Thank you, my dear little house! I like to hear your sweet voice! I'm coming right in. But first, I must collect some fire-wood to cook my dinner." So the Jackal ran about as fast as he could and dragged all the branches and dry sticks close to the mouth of the den.

The old Alligator kept very still, and smiled as he said to himself, "Aha! At last I will catch that tiresome little Jackal! In a few minutes he will run in here and then won't I snap him up?" And the old Alligator rolled his eyes and smacked his lips and ground his teeth.

Now when the Jackal had piled up all the sticks that he could find, he pushed them close up to the den and set them on fire. And the smoke and flames filled the den and smothered the wicked old Alligator and burned him to a cinder.

The little Jackal danced about the den singing:

"Ring-a-ting-a-ting! How do you like my house, friend Alligator? Is it nice and warm in my house, friend Alligator? The Alligator will trouble me no more! Ding-dong, ding-dong! So I dance and sing! Sing-song, sing-song! My enemy is gone! Ring-a-ting, ting-a-ting, ding, ding, dong!"

THE BOLD BLACKBIRD

Once upon a time a Blackbird and his mate lived happily in a tall tree. The Blackbird kept singing sweetly to his mate, pouring out his heart, as they built their nest together. And when the nest was finished and they settled in it, he sang more sweetly than ever.

Now, the King was riding that way and, when he heard this song of joy, he said to the Fowler: "Catch that Blackbird, so that I may hear his happy song every day."

Not long after that the Fowler came with his nets and, by mistake, he caught Mrs. Blackbird. Now Mrs. Blackbird could sing hardly a note, but the Fowler could not tell her from Mr. Blackbird as both wore such black feathers.

The King was delighted to get the bird and he put her into a cage. But Mrs. Blackbird was so unhappy without her husband that she began to mourn and droop, and gave unhappy little chirps.

The King could not understand why he never heard the glad song of the forest; but he kept her a prisoner, hoping that some day she might sing.

Now, when Mr. Blackbird heard that his dear little wife had been stolen by the King, he was very angry indeed. He made up his mind that he would go to the palace and make war upon the King, demanding that his wife be set free. So, he got a long sharp thorn, and tied it at his waist for a sword. On his head he put half a walnut shell for a helmet. He took the skin of a dead frog and put it on for armor, and the other half of the walnut shell he used for a drum. And so he marched away beating upon his drum to make war upon the King.

As he walked along the road, beating upon his drum, he met a Cat.

"Miaow! Miaow!" said the Cat. "Where are you going, Mr. Blackbird?"

"I am going to fight against the King," answered the bold Blackbird.

"I will go with you and help you," said the Cat, "for the King drowned my kittens, and I should like to help punish him."

"Jump into my ear, then," said the bold Blackbird, "and I will take you with me."

So the Cat climbed into the Blackbird's ear, curled up and went to sleep; the Blackbird marched on beating upon his drum.

Further down the road he met some Ants.

"Where are you going, Mr. Blackbird?" asked the Ants.

"I am going to fight against the King," answered the bold Blackbird, "for he has stolen my wife and shut her up in a cage."

"We will join you," said the Ants, "for the King poured hot water down our hole."

"Jump into my ear," said the Blackbird.

So they jumped in, and away went the Blackbird beating upon his drum.

Next the Blackbird met a Rope and a Club, and when they heard that he was going to fight against the King, they jumped into his ear, and away they all went together.

Not far from the palace of the King, the Blackbird had to cross over a river.

"Where are you going, Mr. Blackbird?" asked the River.

"To fight against the King, for he has taken my wife as prisoner."

"I will join you," said the River.

"Jump into my ear," said the Blackbird. So the River went into his ear, and away they all went to the palace of the King.

When they reached the outer gate, the bold Blackbird knocked loudly: "Thump! Thump! Thump!"

"Who is there?" said the Porter.

"General Blackbird, who has come to make war upon the King and to get his wife back again," said the Blackbird.

When the Porter saw General Blackbird in his frog-skin coat of armor, with his helmet and drum made from a walnut shell, and with a thorn for a sword, he laughed so hard that he could scarcely open the gate. And when the King saw the bold bird, he laughed so heartily he nearly fell from his throne. "Ha! Ha! Ha!" roared the King. "What do you wish with me, bold General Blackbird?"

"I want my wife at once," said the Blackbird, beating upon his drum, rub-a-dub, rub-a-dub!

"You shall not have her! I have shut her up in a cage and I am waiting for her to sing to me," said the King.

"Very well, then," answered the Blackbird. "War is declared and you must take the consequences." Rub-a-dub, rub-a-dub! went the drum.

"Seize that insolent bird," said the King, "and shut him up in the hen-house. There will be nothing left of him in the morning."

So the servants took the Blackbird and threw him out into the hen-house.

When all the world was sound asleep, Blackbird said:

"Come out, Pussy, from my ear!
There are many fowls for you here;
Scratch them—make their feathers fly,
Wring their necks until they die!"

"Miaow! Miaow," said the big Pussy Cat. And in an instant all was wild confusion in the hen-house.

"Cluck-cluck-cluck!" said the Hens, as they went scurrying all over the place. "Bad luck-cluck-cluck!"

"Cock-a-doodle-do-oo! Get out of here, oh, do!" shrieked the Rooster.

"Quack, Quack!" said the Ducks. "Alack, Alack!"

"Hiss-ss! Hiss-ss! What's amiss-ss?" hissed the Geese.

But the big Pussy Cat caught them all, scratched out their feathers, and soon made an end of them. Then she climbed back into the Blackbird's ear, and they all went to sleep.

The next morning, the King said to his servants, "Go and find the body of that insolent bird and give all of my poultry an extra measure of corn."

But when they entered the chicken-yard, there was General Blackbird strutting about among all the dead fowls.

The King was very angry when he heard about this, and he said, "Tonight, you must shut that insolent bird in the stable among my prancing steeds. They will soon kick the life out of him."

So General Blackbird was shut in the stable.

At midnight, when all the world was asleep, Blackbird said:

"Come out, Rope, and come out, Stick!
Tie the horses lest they kick.
Beat the horses on the head!
Beat them till they fall down dead!"

"Ha, ha, ha!" roared the King....
"What do you wish with me, bold General Blackbird?"

Out came the Rope and the Club, and the Rope bound all the horses until they could not move, and the Club beat them until they all fell down dead.

Then the Rope and the Club climbed back into the Blackbird's ear, and they all went to sleep again.

The next morning the King said, "I am sure my wild horses have settled that Blackbird. Go out and bring in his corpse."

The servants went out to the stable, and there was the Blackbird sitting on a stall, drumming away on his walnut shell, while all around him were the dead bodies of the horses. Now these horses had cost the King a great deal of money and to have them killed in this way was more than he could stand.

"That Blackbird shall not trick me again," scolded the King. "I will kill him tonight. Put him in with my Elephants and they will crush the life out of him."

So that night the servants shut the Blackbird up in the shed with all the big Elephants.

At midnight, when all the world was sound asleep, the Blackbird began to sing:

"Come out from my ear, you Ants,
Come and sting the Elephants.
Sting each trunk and sting each head!
Sting them till they fall down dead!"

Then out came the swarm of Ants from the Blackbird's ear. They crawled inside the Elephants' trunks; they burrowed into the Elephants' brains; they bit them and stung them so sharply that the Elephants all went mad and trumpeted wildly as they pushed each other about tramping upon each other until they all fell down dead.

The next morning the King said to his servants, "Go and bring me the proof that the insolent Blackbird is dead."

But, when the servants went out, there they found the Blackbird playing upon his drum, while about him all the dead Elephants were piled upon the ground.

When the King heard this he was furious, and he said, "I cannot imagine how he does this, but, tonight, you must tie him to my bed and I will watch to see what happens."

So that night General Blackbird was escorted to the King's bedroom, and there he was tied fast to the King's bed.

The King would not go to sleep, but kept awake listening to find out what the Blackbird was doing.

At midnight the Blackbird began to sing:

"Come out, River, from my ear!
Flow about the King's room here.
Pour yourself upon his bed!
Drown the King until he's dead!"

Then out came the River, drip-drip-drip, pour-pour-pouring out of the Blackbird's ear. It flooded the room; the chairs and tables began to float about; then the King's bed began to float, and the King himself was wet. At last the King cried out:

"Oh, good General Blackbird, stop the River! I will give you back your wife if you will only be gone and leave me in peace."

So the Blackbird stopped the River, took his wife and they went back to their home.

On the way, the Blackbird took all his helpers out of his ear and put each one back where he lived. Taking off his helmet, he said, with a low bow:

"My friends, my wife and I appreciate and thank you for your timely assistance. Without your aid, I should never have been able to overcome the enemy."

Then the Blackbird threw off his frog-skin coat of armor, put aside his thorn sword, his walnut helmet and his drum, and he and his wife flew back to their home in the tall tree.

He sang her a sweet song, and they all lived happily ever after.

THE KID AND THE TIGER

Once upon a time there lived in the forest a mother goat who had four fat little kids, named Roley, Poley, Skipster and Jumpster.

Not far away from the home of the goats lived a mother tiger with her two little cubs.

Now the mother tiger always pretended to be a dear friend of the Nanny goat, but she really was jealous because Nanny had four little ones while she herself had only two.

One day the old tiger growled to herself, "If only I could find some way to eat up two of Nanny's kids, then all things would be equal. But I must never let Nanny suspect me." So the tricky tiger licked her striped coat until it fairly shone and she went to call on the Nanny goat.

"Dear friend Nanny," she said with a sweet smile, "my little ones have gone out and I am very lonely at home. Do please let one of your dear little kids sleep with me."

"Why, I shall be very glad to have one of them go," answered the stupid goat, for she felt flattered that one of her children should be invited to visit the great tiger.

So Mother Goat went out to find her children. They were all having a frolic together. Roley and Poley were rolling over and over upon the ground, and Jumpster was jumping over Skipster.

"Come, children! Come, children!" called their mother. "A good, kind friend has invited one of you to come and spend the night in her house."

"Ma—aa, Ma—aa," bleated all the kids as they came running up and three of the little kids shouted, "Let me go! Let me! Oh, let me!"

But Roley, who was a wise little kid, said very quietly, "Who is the friend, Mammy?"

"Why, it is your dear Aunt Yellow-Stripe," answered the Mother Goat.

Then all the little kids looked very sad, for they were afraid of the tiger. Although the Mother Tiger always smiled upon them, they could see her glistening teeth and when she tried to shake paws with them, they were afraid of her cruel claws; sometimes, when she rolled her eyes and looked at them, they felt that there was a gleam in her eyes which was not for their good.

"No-oo, thank you, Mammy! I would rather stay at home with you," said Skipster.

"No-oo, No-oo, thank you, Mammy!" said Jumpster.

"No-oo, No-oo, thank you, Mammy!" said Poley.

They looked about at Roley to join in their frolic but, to their great surprise, Roley said, "Yes, Mammy, I will go, gladly."

"Baa-ba-bad. Too bad-baa-baad!" bleated the other three kids. "Oh, don't go, poor Roley, we do not trust that terrible tiger!"

But Roley would not heed their warning. He knew what he was about and he made up his mind that he would not let that terrible tiger trick him.

So Roley went home with the tiger, and although she purred over him and made a great fuss over him, he watched her very sharply.

When it was time to go to bed, Roley pretended to go to sleep, but he was watching all the time. At last he heard the old tiger snoring. He got up as softly as he could and went to the back of the den and found one of the baby tigers. They had not gone out as their mother had said, but were sleeping in a dark corner.

Roley took the little tiger-cub and put it down by the Mother Tiger, then he went and hid by the other little tiger.

About midnight the old Mother Tiger awoke and felt the little warm thing curled up by her side. Then she brought down her powerful paw with such force that she killed the little one at once, and gobbled him up. It was so pitchy black that she did not know, until morning, that she had eaten one of her own babies by mistake, for there was little Roley on the floor playing with her other little one.

When she realized what had happened she was wild with rage. Her eyes gleamed with a cruel light, but she managed to purr out sweetly, "Did you sleep well last night, Roley dear?"

"Yes, Auntie," said Roley, "only a gnat stung me."

"Well, never mind," she murmured. "Just come again tonight and we shall see what we shall see."

That night everything happened just as before; only Roley put a huge stone in his place, and then he ran for home as fast as he could go.

At midnight, when the tiger awoke, she brought down her paw upon the stone.

"Did you sleep well last night, Roley dear?"

"My gracious," she said, "but that is a strong kid. I must kill him now, or he will kill me when he grows up." So she bit at the stone with all her might—and broke all her front teeth. Howling with rage and pain, she looked all about her den, but Roley was not to be found.

Mother Tiger lay awake all night with the pain in her teeth. She thought and thought, but she could not plan her revenge upon Roley. So, in the morning, she went to a wise old, one-eyed tiger, her friend and counsellor, and asked him how she could punish Roley.

They talked and they walked and they walked and they talked and when they came back to the den, there was the reckless Roley, rolling about with the little tiger cub.

"Ha, ha," laughed the old tiger. "So here you are, you little rascal! Just sit down and I will tell you a nice story."

"Oh, do, dear Uncle One-eye," cried Roley.

So One-Eye began, "When I eat my dinner, I like to eat kids. Four little kids are just one mouthful for me, and today I'm very hungry. So I am coming to your house and I shall make one mouthful of you and your brothers and sisters."

"Good, good!" cried Roley, clapping his paws. "What good stories you do tell. Now, listen, and I will tell you a story.

"When you come to eat us up, Skipster will hold you by the forelegs, and Jumpster will hold you by the hind legs, and Poley will hold your head, and Roley will chop it off. And our mother will have a big fire ready, and we will cook you. But I think first we will skin off your coat for it will make us such a nice striped rug for our floor."

This story terrified the old tiger and he took to his heels and ran for home as fast as he could go.

On the way home, he met six other tigers and he said, "My dear friends, I know where there's a fine kid for you to eat. I do not care for him, myself, but I will help you catch him, and I will watch you eat him."

The six tigers were all so hungry that each one would have liked to eat the whole kid. As they followed One-Eye, each tiger was plotting how to make the others do the work so that he could get the kid.

They started toward the goat's home and, sure enough, there was Roley, rolling along toward home. But the minute he saw the tigers he crawled up into a tall tree that grew near his house.

The first tiger gave a spring in the air, but could not reach the branch where Roley was sitting. Then the second tiger tried. And, one after another, each tiger jumped, but missed Roley. So he sat there on his perch, mocking them: "Baa-ba—too baad! too bad!"

At last the tigers had to give up and they all sat in a ring and took counsel together. Then One-Eye said, "I know how we can reach him. I will stand here against the tree trunk and the rest of you can climb on my back, one on top of the other. Then we can catch the rascal very easily."

They all agreed that this was an excellent plan. So One-Eye propped himself against the tree, and the other tigers climbed one on top of the other, until the top tiger reached out his paw and almost touched Roley. As he did so, One-Eye cocked up his eye to see how they were getting along.

Roley called out, "Mother, oh, Mother, give me a lump of mud, and I will hit the old brute in his one eye, and that will finish him."

When One-Eye heard this he was so frightened that he gave a great jump and down tumbled the whole seven tigers in a heap, and all fighting and biting and scratching and spitting at each other, for they imagined other beasts were fighting them, and so they fought with one another until they were quite worn out.

As soon as each of the seven tigers got his four legs to himself, off he went to his home.

Then Roley climbed down from the tree and all those joyous kids kicked up their heels and rejoiced together.

Although they never had a tiger skin rug for their floor, they were just as happy, for they did not care to be reminded of their tricky friend, Yellow-Stripe. And the terrible tigers were so frightened that they never again troubled Nanny Goat and her four frolicsome kids.

THE BRAHMIN AND THE TIGER

Once upon a time there lived in India a very good man. He was a Brahmin, or priest, and he had such a kind heart that he could not bear to see anything suffer. Everyone loved him, because he was so good to all the poor people and so gentle with the beasts.

One day, as the Brahmin was walking along the road, he saw a huge Tiger who had been caught by the villagers and put in an iron cage to punish him for his wickedness.

"Brother Brahmin, Brother Brahmin," moaned the Tiger, "pray have pity on me and let me out of this cruel cage for one little minute, so that I may get a drink of water for I am dying of thirst."

"Oh, no, Brother Tiger," answered the Brahmin, "I could not do that, for you are being punished for your wickedness. Moreover if I should let you out of your cage, you would eat me up."

"In truth, I would not," answered the Tiger. "I would never do such an ungrateful thing. Have pity on me, kind Brother Brahmin, I pray!"

Then the Brahmin, feeling sorry for the Tiger, unlocked the cage door. But the moment he opened the door, the Tiger sprang out upon him, growling, "Gurr! gurr! gurr-r-r! Now I will eat you first and drink the water afterwards."

"Why, Brother Tiger!" said the Brahmin, "do not kill me so hastily. You promised not to eat me, and now, when I set you free, you break your word. Is that fair, or just? Is that according to the law?"

"Gurr! gurr! gurr-r-r!" growled the Tiger. "I care not whether it is fair or just. I learned no law in the jungle. Man is the food for the beast."

"But, Brother Tiger, you must listen to reason," said the Brahmin. "We will ask six judges if you are keeping your word to me, and if each one of them says that you should kill me, then I am willing to die."

"Very well," agreed the Tiger, "we will ask the judgment of six and if they all say that you are to die, I shall kill you, but if anyone of them grants you your life, I will have to let you go."

So the Brahmin and the Tiger walked to a Banyan tree, and the Brahmin said:

"Oh, Banyan tree, Banyan tree, hear and give judgment!"

"On what must I give judgment?" asked the Banyan tree.

"This Tiger was caught in a cruel cage," said the Brahmin. "He was thirsty and begged piteously for a drink of water. He promised not to hurt me if I set him free. But when I did so, he sprang upon me to kill me. Do you think it fair and just for him to break his word?"

The Banyan tree rustled his leaves and whispered in a mournful voice, "Men take shelter under my boughs from the scorching rays of the sun. Yet when I have protected them and they are rested, they break my pretty branches and scatter my leaves and take my fruit. Men certainly are an ungrateful race! So I say let the Tiger eat the Brahmin."

"Now, Brother Brahmin," growled the Tiger, "I shall eat you."

"One moment, Brother Tiger," begged the Brahmin. "We agreed to ask six judges, and we have had the opinion of only one. You must not eat me yet."

"Very well," said the Tiger, and they went on till they met a Camel.

"Brother Camel, Brother Camel," cried the Brahmin. "Hear and give judgment." The Brahmin then told how he had opened the cage door for the Tiger and how the Tiger had broken his word. "Do you call that just, or right, Brother Camel?" asked the Brahmin.

"As just and right as I am treated by man," snorted the Camel, gnashing his teeth in rage. "When I was young and strong and could carry a heavy load for my master, he took care of me and gave me food and shelter. Now I am old and have lost my strength in the service, and so he overloads me, starves me and beats me. Men are an unjust and cruel race. So I say let the Tiger eat the Brahmin."

"Now, Brother Brahmin," growled the Tiger, "I shall eat you." And he sprang towards the Brahmin.

"Stop! Brother Tiger, stop!" said the Brahmin. "We have heard only the judgment of two."

"Very well," answered the Tiger.

At a little distance they found a poor old Bullock, lying by the side of the road.

"Brother Bullock, Brother Bullock," said the Brahmin. "Hear and give judgment." Then the Brahmin explained the whole story again and said, "Do you call that fair or just?"

"Brother Camel, Brother Camel," cried the Brahmin....
"Hear and give judgment."

"When I was able to work," answered the Bullock, "my master fed me and treated me very carefully. Now I am old, he has forgotten all I ever did for him and has left me by the roadside to die. Men show no mercy to the beasts. So I say, let the Tiger eat the Brahmin."

"You hear that, Brother Brahmin?" growled the Tiger. "Now I shall eat you up."

"Pray, Brother Tiger, have patience! We have met only half of our judges. I still have three more to ask."

"Very well," answered the Tiger, and they went on together.

After a time they saw an Eagle flying through the air. "Brother Eagle, Brother Eagle," shouted the Brahmin, "fly down here and give judgment."

The Eagle came soaring slowly down and sat upon a rock. Then the Brahmin told his whole story and said, "Do you think that it is fair, or just of the Tiger to eat me after I set him free?"

"Well," answered the Eagle, "men are not fair nor just to me. Whenever men see me, they try to shoot me and they climb the rocks to spoil my nest and steal my little ones. Men know no pity. They seek only to slay us. So I say let the Tiger eat the Brahmin."

"Hear that, Brother Brahmin? Now I shall have to kill you," growled the Tiger.

"Have patience, Brother Tiger," answered the Brahmin. "We have yet two more judges to ask."

"Very well," said the Tiger, and they went on their way.

Presently they came to a river and in the mud they saw an old Alligator. The Brahmin told him the whole story hoping that the Alligator would give him a favorable answer. But the Alligator in great anger snorted out:

"Humph! I hunt no man, but, whenever I put my nose out of the water, men torment me and try to kill me. As long as men live, we shall have no peace. So I say let the Tiger eat the Brahmin."

Then the Tiger, sprang toward the Brahmin. "This time I shall eat you up, for all are against you."

"One moment!" said the Brahmin. "I still have one opinion of the sixth judge."

So the Tiger was obliged to wait, and by and by they met a little Jackal who came gaily prancing down the road.

"Oh, Brother Jackal! dear little Brother Jackal," called the Brahmin, "please do stop a minute and give judgment."

"On what must I give judgment?" barked the little Jackal.

Again the Brahmin told his story and asked, "Do you think it just, or fair that the Tiger should eat me up after I set him free from that cruel cage?"

"Cage, cage, cage?" asked the little Jackal in a perplexed tone. "I don't quite understand. What sort of cage was it?"

"Why, a big iron cage down in the village," answered the Brahmin. "The men had caught the Tiger to punish him for his wickedness. When I came down the road he begged for a drink of water and promised he would not eat me, if I set him free. But when I opened the cage-door, he sprang upon me to kill me. Do you call that fair, or just?"

"Dear me, dear me!" said the little Jackal. "How can I decide who is right or wrong until I see the cage and the exact position you were in when the quarrel began? Show me the place and I will try to judge."

So the Brahmin and the Tiger and the little Jackal went back to the place where the empty cage stood.

"Oh, is that the cage?" asked the Jackal.

"Yes, yes," answered the Brahmin.

"Well, Brahmin, show me exactly where you stood," said the Jackal.

"Here," said the Brahmin. "I stood here in the road looking in the cage at the cruel Tiger."

"Where were you, Tiger?" asked the Little Jackal.

"Why, I stood in the cage, so!" answered the Tiger jumping into the cage, "and my head was leaning against the iron bars, so!"

"Very good, very good!" said the little Jackal. "But I cannot give judgment until I understand a little more. Why did you not come out by yourself, Tiger? Was the cage-door open, or shut?"

"Why, the cage-door was shut and bolted!" answered the Brahmin.

"Then shut and bolt it," said the Jackal, "for I must see how all this happened."

The Brahmin shut and bolted the cage-door and, turning to the Jackal, he said, "Now give us your judgment, Brother Jackal."

"Ha-ha-ha!" barked the little Jackal, joyously. "Leave it locked! Leave it locked, Brother Brahmin! Oh, you wicked and ungrateful Tiger! After the good Brahmin was kind enough to open the cage-door, was it fair, or just, for you to spring upon him to kill him? You may stay in that cage all the rest of your life. Goodbye, Brother Brahmin, goodbye," said the little Jackal. "My way leads this way and your way leads that. Goodbye!"

And away ran the little Jackal in one direction while Brother Brahmin went on his way, rejoicing that he was safe. And shut up in the cage, the old Tiger roared in a rage.

THE BEAR'S BAD BARGAIN

Once upon a time there lived an old woodman and his wife in a tiny little hut near the edge of the forest. Now, a very rich man had his orchard near their home—so close, in fact, that the boughs of a big pear-tree hung right over their yard. The rich man was a generous neighbor, and he agreed to give the poor man and his wife the fruit that fell into their garden. So the old woodman and his wife watched with hungry eyes as the pears ripened in the sunshine.

"How I wish that a wind-storm would come and let those pears drop on our side of the fence," said the old woman.

"Yes," agreed the old man; "I wish that I dared to shake the tree a little and make some of the fruit fall this way, but our neighbor might see it, and then he would be angry and not give us any of them."

Every day, the old woman grumbled more and more, because the pears did not drop on their side of the fence.

"I declare, we shall be beggars," she groaned; and she insisted that her husband work harder and harder each day, while she would give him nothing to eat but a dry crust of bread.

The poor man grew thinner and thinner while he waited for the pears to ripen and fall into their yard; and every day he worked harder and harder, but he could not please his grumbling old wife. At last he turned around on her and, in great anger, said, "Wife, I will not do any more work unless you make some khichri for my dinner."

"Khichri!" shrieked the wife; "khichri! Indeed I will not. Do you not know that khichri takes rice and pulse and butter and spices? Do you think that I am going to use all we have in the house on one meal for you?"

"Yes," said the old man, "that is why I demand khichri. You have starved me quite long enough and now I will have the best dish you can make me."

The cross old woman took the things out of the closet and began to cook a savory khichri. It smelt so good that the old man could hardly wait for it.

"Let me have a taste?" he begged.

"No, no," scolded his wife, "you cannot have even a taste of it until you have brought me in another load of wood, and mind that it is a big one. You will have to work for your khichri."

The old woodman took his axe and went out to the forest and began to hew and hack the trees with all his strength and soon he had a large load of wood.

Chop! chop! chop! At every blow of his axe he would think of the savory khichri he would soon enjoy.

Suddenly a big black bear came lumbering along through the forest with his long black nose tilted in the air and his little keen eyes peering all about him, for bears are always curious.

"Grr-rr-Grr-rr! Good-day to you, my friend," growled the bear. "And may I ask what you are doing with that large bundle of wood?"

"I cut it for my wife," answered the woodman. "You see, she would not cook me any dinner unless I brought her the wood. Today she has made me khichri for dinner and I know that when she sees this large load of wood, she will give me a generous portion. Oh, just smell that khichri; it is delicious!"

This made the bear very hungry and so he growled, "Do you think that your wife would give me some khichri, if I brought her some wood?"

"Maybe she might, if you brought her a very large load," answered the man.

After a long discussion, the bear agreed to bring in half a cord of wood, if the man would save him some of the khichri.

"Half a cord is a very large load of wood," grumbled the bear.

"But there is saffron and rice and pulse and butter in the khichri. It is a very expensive dish," said the woodman.

The bear licked his chops at this and his bright little eyes gleamed with greed.

"It is a bargain," he cried. "I will bring you half a cord of wood, so go home and tell your wife to keep the khichri hot, for I shall be with you soon."

The woodman went home and told his wife about his bargain with the bear. "Half a cord of wood is good pay for a share of our dinner," said the man.

Now the wife knew that her husband had made a good bargain with the bear, but she always found fault and grumbled about everything, so she began to scold the old man.

"You should have made a better bargain with the bear. Bears are always greedy," she stormed. "You know that he will gobble up all the khichri, before we have had a mouthful."

"Do you think your wife would give me some khichri, if I brought her some wood?"

When the woodman heard this he grew quite pale. "Don't you think that we had better begin now and have a fair start before the bear comes?" he asked.

So they squatted down upon the floor mat with the big brass pot of khichri placed between and began to eat and eat as fast as they could.

"Yum-mm, Yum-mm, YUMM, this khichri is good!" mumbled the man as he crammed his mouth full. "But we must remember to leave some for the bear, wife!"

"Yes, certainly, certainly!" replied the woman, helping herself to more. "We must leave some for that poor hungry bear!"

But they went right on eating and eating until there was not a single mouthful left in the pot.

"What shall we do now, when the bear comes?" cried the woodman. "It is all your fault, wife, for suggesting that the bear would eat it all."

"My fault! my fault, indeed!" shrieked the wife. "You suggested that we begin to eat before the bear came in, and you ate twice as much as I did!"

"No, I did not!"

"Yes, you did so, and you know it!"

"Well, there is no good in quarrelling about it now," said the woodman. "The bear will be here in a few moments and he will be furious when he finds the khichri all gone. He is very large and very hungry and he may eat us when he finds that we have gone back on our word."

"Nonsense!" said the woman. "What a coward you are! All you think about is saving yourself! I do not care whether he is angry or not. I want to get that wood from him."

"He will never give it to you, when he finds no dinner," said the man. "Of course not, you stupid," scolded the woman, "but I have thought of a plan. We must lock up everything in the house and leave the khichri pot by the fire, to look as though we were keeping it hot for him and then we must hide in the garret. When the bear comes and does not see us, he will think that we have gone out and left his dinner for him; then he will throw down his wood and come in. When he finds that the pot is empty, he will rampage about a little, but he cannot do very much damage. He will never bother to carry all that wood away again, for bears are as lazy as they are greedy."

Now all this time the bear had been working hard in the forest and it took him much longer than he had expected to gather all that wood. However, at last he dragged half a cord of wood to the house of the old woodman. Seeing the brass khichri pot standing by the fire, he threw down his pile of wood and went at once for his dinner. And then when he saw that there was not even a grain of rice left in the pot, Me-oh-my! wasn't he angry? He growled and he roared and he poked his head 'way down into the pot and licked the sides of it. But not even a tiny bit of pulse could he taste, though all the time he could smell how savory that khichri had been.

He sat on the floor and cried in his rage and disappointment, "Grr-rr! Grr! Grr-rr-rr! That is a fine way to keep a promise! Well, since you have eaten all the khichri, I will find something else to eat!" Then he upset everything in the house, but no food could he find.

"Grr! Grr-rr! Grr-rr!" growled the bear. "I will take all of this wood back to the forest again. They broke their bargain with me and they shall not have one of my sticks to burn."

But just as the old woman had expected he was much too lazy to carry the heavy load back to the forest, even for revenge.

"I will not go away empty-handed," he growled. "If they would not save me a taste, I can at least get the smell!" And he carried the brass pot away with him.

Now, as the bear left the cottage, he saw the beautiful golden pears hanging from the tree. These were the first pears of the season, and they looked very good to him. So he climbed up into the tree and began to eat the biggest, ripest pear that he could find. My! but it was good! The bear was so hungry, after his hard work in the forest, that he licked his chops and smacked his lips as he munched the pear. And then he thought of a plan.

"I shall take these pears home with me and sell them to the other bears in the forest and with the money I can buy all the khichri that I can eat! Ha! Ha! Ha!" laughed the bear. "I shall have the best of the bargain after all! I will fool that old woodman and his wife, and they will not have even so much as a taste of one."

Then the bear began to gather the ripe pears as fast as he could and put them into the big brass pot, but whenever he came to an unripe pear he would shake his head and say, "No one will buy this green one, yet it is a shame to waste it." So he would pop the green pear into his own mouth and gobble it up, though he made wry faces as he ate.

Now all this time, the woodman and his wife had been hiding in the garret and the woodman's wife was peeking through a little crevice watching the bear. When she saw how furious he was, she held her breath for fear he would discover them. When he climbed the tree and was eating the pears, she was angry at losing their share of the fruit, but she was too terrified to call out. At last from the excitement and the dust in her hiding place, she could hold in no longer, and just when the bear had filled the pot with ripe golden pears, out she came with a most tremendous sneeze: "A-h Che-u! Che-uu-uu!"

The bear was startled by this sound—so much like the explosion of a gun—and off he lumbered into the forest, dropping the khichri pot in the yard as he ran.

Now, as the pot had dropped into their yard, the woodman and his wife got all the pears, as well as the khichri they had eaten, and half a cord of wood, while the poor bear got nothing but a very bad stomachache from eating unripe fruit. So that was the end of the bear's bad bargain.

THE MAN WHO RODE A TIGER

Once upon a time, in a terrible thunderstorm, a big Tiger crept for shelter close to the wall of an old woman's hut. Now, this old woman was very poor. Her hut was a tumbledown old place, and the rain leaked through the holes in her roof.

"Drip-drip-drip," fell the rain, and the poor old woman tried to drag her furniture away from the holes in the roof.

"Oh, dear, oh, dear!" she moaned. "What an awful storm! I'm sure I would not be nearly as afraid of a big tiger, or an elephant, or a lion, as I am of this perpetual dripping—dripping." And she dragged her bed across the room to get it away from the dripping water.

The Tiger, crouching against the house, heard every word. "This perpetual dripping that frightens her more than a tiger, or an elephant, or a lion, must be very terrible," he said. "What can this perpetual dripping be?"

And, then, as he heard her dragging the things about in the house, he said, "My, what a horrible noise! Surely that noise must be perpetual dripping."

Now, at this moment, a Chattee-maker (potter) came down the road. The night was very cold. His donkey had strayed away, and the poor old man was so bewildered that he could not find the donkey. Suddenly there was a flash of lightning and the man saw a large beast lying by the wall of the old woman's hut.

Mistaking the beast for his donkey, the Chattee-maker rushed at the Tiger, seized it by the ear and commenced beating and abusing it with all his might.

"You wretched old donkey, you, to run away and leave me to look for you in this frightful storm! Get up and carry me home, or I'll break every bone in your lazy old body!" He kicked the poor beast and pounded him.

"Look, look!" they cried in terror....
"Here comes a man of gigantic stature, riding on a mighty horse."

The Tiger did not know what to make of it. He was very much frightened. "This must be 'Perpetual Dripping,'" he said to himself. "No wonder the old woman said she was more afraid of it than of a tiger, or an elephant, or a lion, for it gives so many hard blows."

As soon as the poor Tiger got up, the Chattee-maker climbed on his back and forced the Tiger to carry him home. All the way he kicked and beat the Tiger, thinking it was his donkey. When he got home, the Chattee-maker tied the Tiger securely to the hitching-post in front of the house, and went in to bed.

Next morning, when the Chattee-maker's wife got up and looked out of her window, she beheld a great Tiger tied up in front of the house. The Tiger looked as frightened and as meek as a lamb.

"Husband! Husband!" she called, loudly. "Wake up! Wake up! Do you know what animal you brought home, last night?"

"Why, yes—my donkey, to be sure," he answered. "The donkey ran away from me, but I caught him just the same, and made him bring me home."

"Come and see for yourself," said his wife.

Here was the great Tiger tied to the post.

"Where is my donkey, then?" asked the man. "I rode him home, last night, and tied him to the post, myself."

"No, you must have ridden on that Tiger," said his wife.

Soon the news spread all over the village that the Chattee-maker had captured a great Tiger and had ridden home on his back, and that he had tied him to his hitching-post and trained him to be as meek as a lamb.

The report was even carried to the Rajah of the country, and he came, with his lords and attendants, to see this astonishing sight.

Now the Tiger was a very large one and had long been the terror of the whole country, and the Rajah was so pleased to have this terrible Tiger captured that he conferred all possible honor on the valiant Chattee-maker.

"You are a very brave man, my friend," said the Rajah. "I will give you a new house and lands. You shall be a lord in my court and you shall be commander of a thousand horsemen."

So the Chattee-maker gave up making pots and clay earthenware and he and his wife lived in the beautiful house given him by the Rajah, and they wore gorgeous raiment. And the Chattee-maker did, indeed, look like a lord of the court.

Wherever he went, people pointed him out and said, "There is the brave man who captured a hungry tiger and rode on his back."

Now, not long after this, a Rajah from a neighboring country sent word that he was bringing a mighty army to wage war. When the people heard this, they were terrified; all the generals came to the Rajah and said, "We are not prepared for war! Who will be the Chief Commander?"

Then some of the people said, "You have just given the Chattee-maker command over a thousand horsemen. He is a brave and fearless man. Why do you not put him in command of your army?"

"That is a very good idea," answered the Rajah. "I will make him Commander-in-Chief."

So he sent for the valiant Chattee-maker. Said he, "My generals are afraid to take command for they say we are not prepared for war, but I know that you are brave and fearless, and into your hands I will place all the power in my kingdom. You must put our enemies to flight."

"It shall be as you command," said the Chattee-maker. "But before I lead the whole army, let me go out alone and find out something about the strength of the enemy, and examine their position."

The Rajah consented to this and the Chattee-maker went home to his wife. "Oh, wife, wife, what shall I do?" he asked, in fright. "They have made me their Commander-in-Chief! It is a very hard place for me to fill. I shall have to ride at the head of my troops, and you know that I was never on a horse in my life. So I have asked the Rajah to let me go out alone first. We shall get a very quiet pony and I shall ride out before anyone sees me."

But, early the next day, before the Chattee-maker had time to start, the Rajah sent to him a very spirited horse, all saddled and bridled, and requested that the Chattee-maker ride that horse out to meet the enemy.

The poor Chattee-maker was terrified, for the horse was a powerful animal that pranced about, champing his bit and rolling his eyes, and the Chattee-maker was sure that, if he ever mounted upon that horse, he would soon fall off. But he did not dare to refuse the horse sent by the Rajah. So he bowed politely to the messengers and said, "Tell the Rajah I am deeply grateful for his gift."

But, when the messengers were gone, he said to his wife, "Oh, oh, what am I to do? How can I ever ride on this terrible horse?"

"Now, do not be so frightened," said his wife. "I will tie you on the back of the big horse and, if you start at night, no one will see that you are tied on."

That night his wife held the horse while her husband jumped and jumped, trying to get up into the saddle. At last, after many trials, he succeeded in getting on. He was so frightened that he called loudly to his wife, "Oh, wife, wife, hurry, hurry!"

So she wound him all about with strong ropes and tied his feet firmly in the stirrups, and she put one rope around his neck and shoulders and around his waist, and fastened them to the saddle.

"Wife, wife," he screamed. "You forgot to tie my hands."

"Oh, no," she said. "It is better for you to have your hands free. Hold on by the mane!"

So he caught the horse's mane as firmly as he could, and away and away went the horse, carrying the poor frightened Chattee-maker. Faster and faster, over hedges and rivers and ditches and plains, he galloped, and galloped, until they came in sight of the enemy's camp.

When the poor old Chattee-maker saw the horse carrying him towards the enemy, he was more frightened than ever.

He made one last effort to save himself and, as the horse darted under a young banyan tree, he stretched out his hand and seized the tree with all his might, hoping that his ropes would break and the tree would pull him down from the horse. But the banyan tree was in very loose soil and the horse was plunging at such terrific speed that, when the Chattee-maker caught hold, up came the tree by the roots, and the Chattee-maker rode on, waving the banyan tree over his head and shrieking and screaming in his fright.

Now the soldiers of the enemy had heard that an army was coming out against them and when they saw the Chattee-maker they were sure he was the leader of a vanguard.

"Look! Look!" they cried in terror. "Here comes a man of gigantic stature, riding on a mighty horse! He rides at full speed over rocks and ditches and tears up the trees in his rage!"

And running to the Rajah, they cried out in fright, "Here comes the whole force of the enemy! Men of gigantic stature, mounted on mighty horses. As they gallop along, they tear up trees in their rage and brandish them about as war-clubs. We can fight men, but we cannot fight monsters!"

Now, the Chattee-maker was coming nearer and nearer and shrieking louder and louder in his terror, as he waved the tree wildly about his head and the horse plunged on.

So others rushed to the Rajah and said, "It is true! It is true! See, they are coming! Look, look! Let us fly for our lives!"

Then the whole panic-stricken crowd fled from their camp, for no one wanted to meet such an enemy. But, first, they made the Rajah write a note, begging for peace.

Soon after the enemy had fled from the camp, the horse carrying the Chattee-maker came galloping into it. As he reached the camp, the ropes broke and the Chattee-maker tumbled to the ground and the horse, worn out from his long run, stood still.

The Chattee-maker looked all about and was greatly surprised to find the whole camp deserted. In the tent of the Rajah he found the letter, and took it back home with him. He was afraid to mount the horse again, so he walked all the long journey back, leading his tired horse.

He did not get home until late that night, but his wife saw him coming, and ran out to meet him.

"Why, what is the matter, my good man?" she asked.

"Oh, wife! wife!" he groaned, "I am so weary! Every bone in my body aches. I have ridden all over the world since last night and I have had to walk all the way back today, and I am so tired and hungry. When I came to the camp of the enemy, no one was there, but I found this letter." Then he told his wife the whole story of his wild ride.

"We must send a messenger to the Rajah with this letter and tell him that you will come in the morning and report for yourself," she said. "We must send the horse, also, for I know that you never want to ride him again."

So his good wife sent the horse and the letter to the Rajah, with the message that her husband would surely come, in the early morning.

And the next day, when the people saw the Chattee-maker walking to the royal palace, they said, "Why, this man is as modest as he is brave. He went out all alone, and put our enemy to flight, and now he walks simply to the door of the Rajah as though he had no pride."

The Rajah came to the palace door to greet the Chattee-maker and, when the Chattee-maker bowed down before the Rajah, the Rajah lifted him to his feet and gave him every honor.

"You have saved our lives and shall be set over all the kingdom," said the Rajah. "You shall be next to me in authority, for you are as modest and as humble as you are brave."

So the Chattee-maker was rewarded for all that he had done by having twice as much rank and wealth given him.

But the Chattee-maker never would ride on a horse. He had his own beautiful coach in which to ride and he was often carried about on a litter so that no one ever knew that he was not a bold and brave rider. Had he not ridden on a tiger and had he not routed an army by rushing at them and pulling up trees to frighten them away? Yes, indeed, the people were all very proud of the valiant Chattee-maker, and he lived very happily, all the rest of his life.

9 789358 007466

Printed by Libri Plureos GmbH in Hamburg,
Germany